HORSING AROUND

RACING HORSES

By Therese Shea

Gareth Stevens
Publishing

Please visit our Web site, www.garethstevens.com. For a free color catalog of all our high-quality books, call toll free 1-800-542-2595 or fax 1-877-542-2596.

Library of Congress Cataloging-in-Publication Data

Shea, Therese.
Racing horses / Therese Shea.
    p. cm. – (Horsing around)
Includes index.
 ISBN 978-1-4339-4636-3 (pbk.)
 ISBN 978-1-4339-4637-0 (6-pack)
 ISBN 978-1-4339-4635-6 (library binding)
1. Horse racing–Juvenile literature. 2. Race horses–Juvenile literature. I. Title.
SF335.6.S54 2011
798.4–dc22

                                    2010031419

First Edition

Published in 2011 by
Gareth Stevens Publishing
111 East 14th Street, Suite 349
New York, NY 10003

Copyright © 2011 Gareth Stevens Publishing

Designer: Michael J. Flynn
Editor: Therese Shea

Photo credits: Cover, pp. 1, (cover, back cover, p. 1 wooden sign), (pp. 2–4, 6–8, 11–12, 15–16, 19–24 wood background), back cover (wood background), 9, 14 Shutterstock.com; p. 5 Andy Lyons/Getty Images; p. 7 Buyenlarge/Archive Photos/ Getty Images; p. 10 Warren Little/Getty Images; p. 13 Matthew Stockman/Getty Images; p. 17 Jerry Cooke/Sports Illustrated/Getty Images; pp. 18–19 Herb Scharfman/ Sports Imagery/Getty Images; p. 20 Donald Miralle/Getty Images.

Printed in the United States of America

CPSIA compliance information: Batch #CW11GS: For further information contact Gareth Stevens, New York, New York at 1-800-542-2595.

For Dad, Mom, and Here-Kitty-Kitty-Kitty, probably still rounding the track

Contents

Words in the glossary appear in **bold** type the first time they are used in the text.

The Sport of Kings

Horse racing has long been called the "sport of kings." It has changed little over thousands of years. Quite simply, the first horse that crosses the finish line wins! Today, many horses line up on a racetrack. They step into starting gates. The gates fly open at the same time, and . . . they're off!

Horses are specially chosen for racing. They're trained over several years. If all goes well, one day they'll find their way to the winner's circle after a big race.

Smarty Jones, ridden by Stewart Elliott, crosses the finish line to win the 2004 Kentucky Derby.

THE MANE FACT

Most European racetracks are turf, or grass. In North America, most tracks are dirt.

5

Harness Racing

There are two kinds of horse racing. One is harness racing. In this sport, a horse pulls a two-wheeled cart with a driver around a track. The cart is called a sulky.

Harness-racing horses are a **breed** called Standardbred. They have long bodies and strong, sturdy legs. They're known for their **endurance**. The most famous harness horse was Dan Patch. He never lost a race. He set a world record for fastest mile in 1905—1 minute 55 seconds!

THE MANE FACT

Dan Patch was so famous that people bought strands of his hair for $5 a piece!

Songs were written to honor Dan Patch, such as "Dan Patch Two Step."

In the other kind of horse racing, a rider sits in a saddle on top of the horse. It's called "racing on the flat."

One type of racing on the flat is quarter-horse racing. These races got their name because they were once only a quarter of a mile (400 m) long. Now quarter-horse races are different lengths. Quarter horses are very **muscular**.

All other races on the flat are run by Thoroughbreds. Thoroughbreds are tall and slim with long necks. They're faster than Standardbreds and quarter horses.

THE MANE FACT

Modern Thoroughbreds are traced to one of three horses brought to England between 1689 and 1730. Their names were the Byerly Turk, the Darley Arabian, and the Godolphin Barb.

8

Many racetracks are built in an oval shape and are about 1 mile (1.6 km) long.

9

Irish Raptor, ridden by Paddy Brennan, clears a tall fence at the 2010 Grand National.

THE MANE FACT

Steeplechases got their name because people once raced toward church towers, called steeples. They were used as end points because they could be seen from far away.

10

Thoroughbred Races

Some races on the flat, such as the **steeplechase**, include jumping. The most famous steeplechase is the Grand National. With fences and ditches as **obstacles**, this English race has been held since 1839.

In the United States, 3-year-old Thoroughbreds run in the most famous races. These races require no jumps, just speed. They are the Kentucky Derby, the Preakness, and the Belmont Stakes. A horse that wins all three in 1 year wins the Triple Crown. No horse has done this since 1978.

Training

Horses naturally love to run. However, they don't know when to speed up, where to place themselves in a pack, and what a finish line is. Racing horses need training.

Trainers create a plan for each horse. That plan includes exercise, the right food, and an understanding of what the horse can do. A trainer prepares each horse for success. However, the trainer isn't in the saddle on race day. A horse's trainer or owner hires a **jockey**.

Jockeys usually ride in a crouching position.

THE MANE FACT

The colors worn by jockeys in races are the colors of the owner or trainer.

13

Jockeys are usually short and thin because horses carrying less weight run faster.

A Jockey's Job

Thoroughbreds can run about a quarter of a mile (400 m) at top speed. Most races are longer than this distance. A jockey paces a horse so it has strength to finish first. Some racing horses like to lead the whole time. Others like to hang back and then turn on the speed. Jockeys must know their horses well.

Some horses respond to a jockey urging, "Hurry up!" Others respond to their jockey's legs pressing into their sides. Some jockeys use **whips**.

THE MANE FACT

There are rules about using whips in races. Some whips are made so that the horse doesn't feel pain when hit.

15

Man o' War

Perhaps the greatest racing horse ever was Man o' War. Racing in 1919 and 1920, he lost only one race. In that race, Man o' War was turned the wrong way at the starting line when the race began. Amazingly, he still got second place!

Sometimes horses carry more or less weight to give other horses a chance to win. This is called a handicap. Usually, the difference is a few pounds. In one race, Man o' War took first place carrying 30 pounds (14 kg) more than the second-place horse!

Man o' War was nicknamed "Big Red."

THE MANE FACT

In a horse race—instead of first place, second place, and third place—horses are said to win, place, and show.

Secretariat (shown here in blue and white) was thirty-fifth on ESPN's 100 Greatest Athletes of the Twentieth Century list.

18

In 1935, Seabiscuit lost 17 races in a row! He was sold to a new owner. Seabiscuit's trainer saw something special in him. In 1938, Seabiscuit ran against Triple Crown champion War Admiral—and won!

However, the "Horse of the Twentieth Century" was Secretariat. He was named Horse of the Year at age 2 in 1972. The next year, he won the Triple Crown. Secretariat won the Belmont Stakes by 31 **lengths** and set a world speed record that still stands.

THE MANE FACT

Seabiscuit was the grandson of Man o' War.

In 2004, Smarty Jones gave racing fans "Smarty Fever"! First, the Thoroughbred proved his skill winning the Kentucky Derby. Then, he won the Preakness by $11\frac{1}{2}$ lengths. All he needed was one more for the Triple Crown.

Smarty Jones and jockey Stewart Elliott easily won the Preakness.

On June 5, the largest crowd ever to watch a New York sports event gathered for the Belmont Stakes. Smarty Jones led most of the way, but finally took second place. Racing fans are still waiting for the next Triple Crown winner. Who will it be?

The Three Races of the Triple Crown

Race	Kentucky Derby	Preakness	Belmont Stakes
Date	first Saturday in May	third Saturday in May	third Saturday after Preakness
Current Track	Churchill Downs	Pimlico Race Course	Belmont Park
Location	Louisville, KY	Baltimore, MD	Elmont, NY
Distance	$1\frac{1}{4}$ miles (2,012 m)	$1\frac{3}{16}$ miles (1,911 m)	$1\frac{1}{2}$ miles (2,414 m)
First Held	1875	1873	1867

Glossary

breed: a group of animals that share features different from others of that kind

endurance: the power to do something hard for a long time

jockey: one who rides racing horses as a job

length: in a horse race, the space between two horses measured by how long a horse is

muscular: having a lot of muscles

obstacle: something that blocks a path

steeplechase: a horse race run over a course that has obstacles horses must jump over

whip: a rod, rope, or strip of leather that is attached to a handle and used to strike an animal

For More Information

Books:

McCarthy, Meghan. *Seabiscuit: The Wonder Horse*. New York, NY: Simon & Schuster Books for Young Readers, 2008.

McKerley, Jennifer Guess. *Man o' War: Best Racehorse Ever*. New York, NY: Random House, 2005.

Sandler, Michael. *Race Horses*. New York, NY: Bearport Publishing, 2007.

Web Sites:

National Museum of Racing and Hall of Fame
www.racingmuseum.org
Read about the best racing horses of all time.

Seabiscuit
www.pbs.org/wgbh/americanexperience/films/seabiscuit/
This PBS site highlighting the achievements of Seabicuit contains a timeline of horse racing in the United States.

23

Index

24